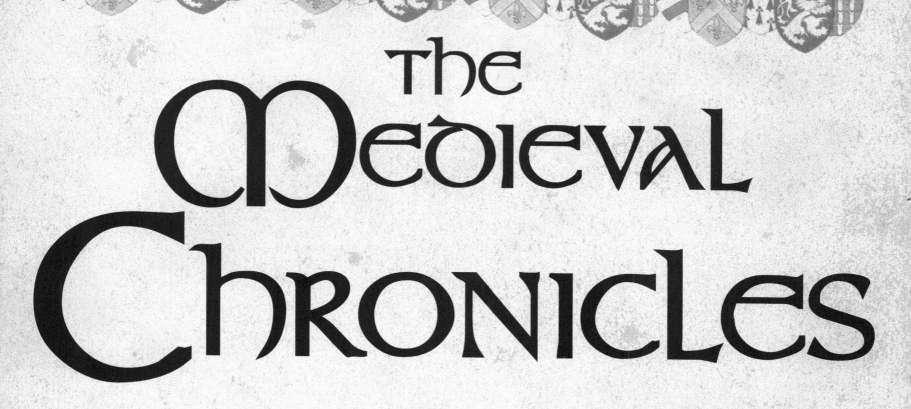

THE MEDIEVAL CHRONICLES

VIKINGS, KNIGHTS, AND CASTLES

Sandy Creek
NEW YORK

An Imprint of Sterling Publishing
387 Park Avenue South
New York, NY 10016

Text © 2013 by The Salariya Book Company Ltd
Illustrations © 2013 by The Salariya Book Company Ltd

This 2013 edition published by Sandy Creek.

Series creator: David Salariya
Authors: Fiona Macdonald, David Stewart, and Derek Farmer
Editor: Stephen Haynes
Illustrations: David Antram, Mark Bergin, Corinne and Ray Burrows,
John James, Mark Peppé, and Carolyn Scrace

ISBN: 978-1-4351-5067-6 (print format)

Manufactured in Heyuan, Guangdong Province, China
Lot #:
2 4 6 8 10 9 7 5 3 1
06/13

CONTENTS

THE VIKING CODEX

Knight: Ready for Battle

The Siege Chronicles

THE VIKING CODEX

INTRODUCTION

Like father, like son! This book tells the story of two great Viking explorers: Erik the Red and his son, Leif the Lucky. They led sailors and settlers across the wild Atlantic Ocean to new homes in faraway lands.

Erik was born in Norway around AD 940. But his family had to leave quickly, in disgrace, "because of some killings."

They escaped to Iceland, where their bold, brave, and bad behavior was remembered by Icelandic storytellers long after they had died. Around AD 1200, their adventures were written down in sagas (exciting epics), and so have survived until today. Read on, and find out more!

AT HOME IN ICELAND

Soon after AD 800, fierce Viking fighting men and peaceful farming families began to sail away from Scandinavia to make new homes overseas. They went in search of land—and to find freedom from newly powerful kings. The first Viking settlers reached Iceland around AD 870. By AD 930, more than 30,000 Viking men, women, and children lived there.

Earl: noble chieftain and war leader

Freeman: rich trader

Slave: foreigner, captured in a raid

Freeman: poor farmer or craftworker

VIKING LANDS

Viking migrants settled over a vast area, from Russia to southern Italy. Viking merchants ventured still farther, to trade in Baghdad and Constantinople (now Istanbul).

NOBLES, FREE PEOPLE, SLAVES

Vikings were not all equal. Free people might be rich or poor, but they had the right to own land and weapons—and the duty to fight for their earl. Slaves belonged to their owners, and had few possessions, but they could buy their freedom or be set free.

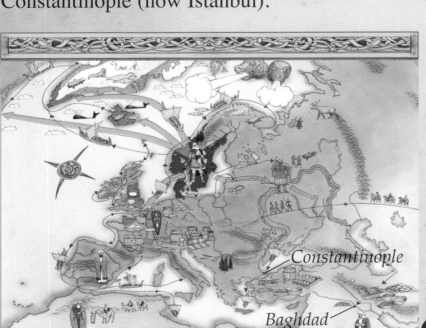

Constantinople

Baghdad

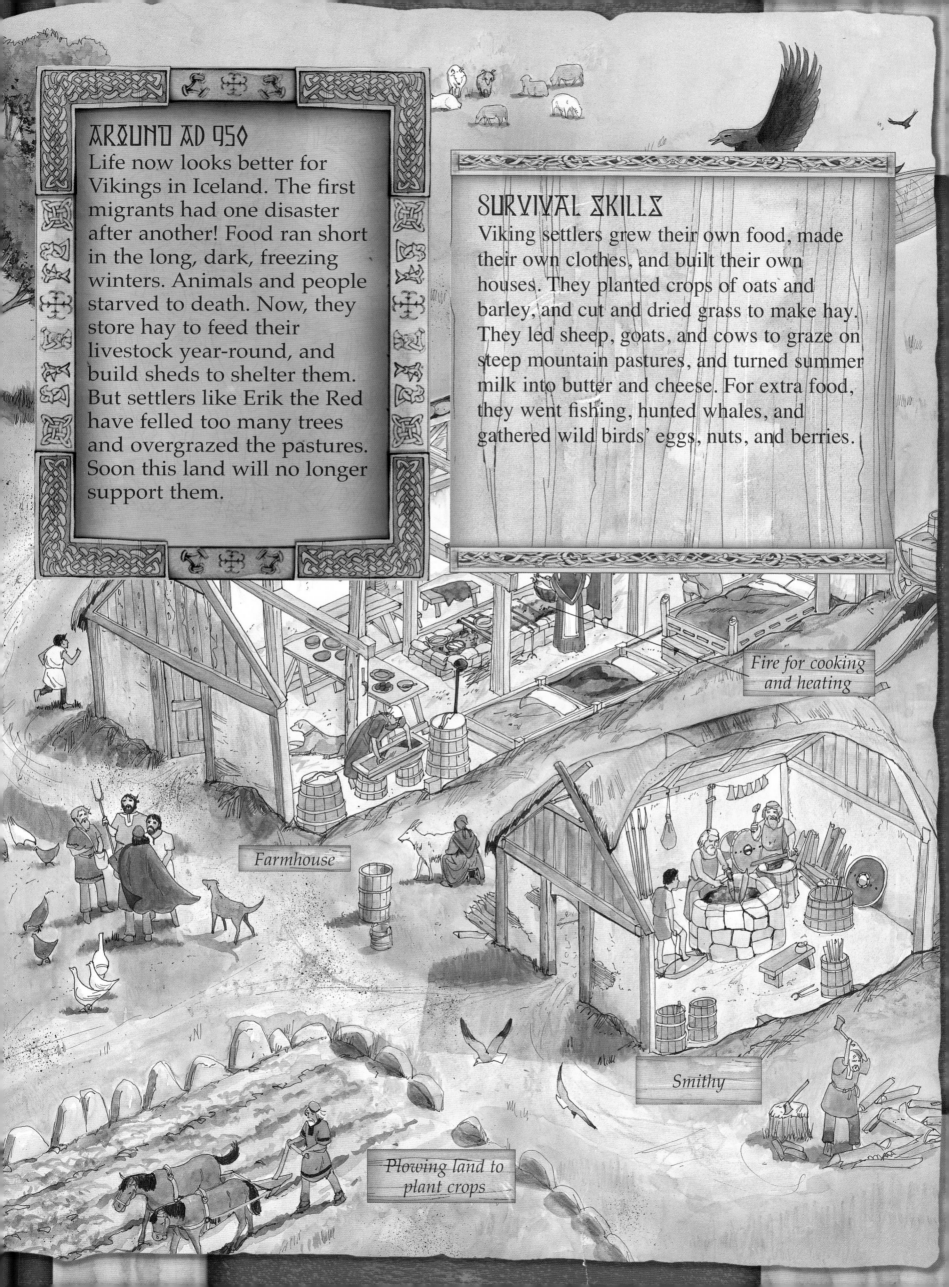

AROUND AD 950

Life now looks better for Vikings in Iceland. The first migrants had one disaster after another! Food ran short in the long, dark, freezing winters. Animals and people starved to death. Now, they store hay to feed their livestock year-round, and build sheds to shelter them. But settlers like Erik the Red have felled too many trees and overgrazed the pastures. Soon this land will no longer support them.

SURVIVAL SKILLS

Viking settlers grew their own food, made their own clothes, and built their own houses. They planted crops of oats and barley, and cut and dried grass to make hay. They led sheep, goats, and cows to graze on steep mountain pastures, and turned summer milk into butter and cheese. For extra food, they went fishing, hunted whales, and gathered wild birds' eggs, nuts, and berries.

Fire for cooking and heating

Farmhouse

Smithy

Plowing land to plant crops

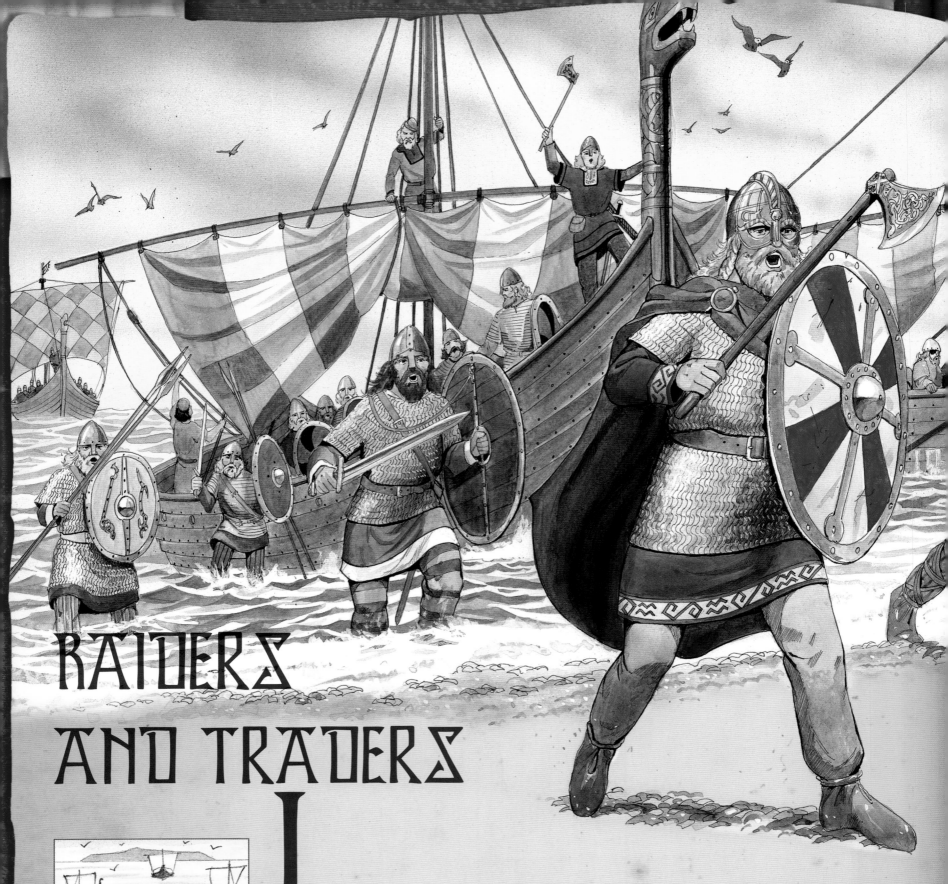

RAIDERS AND TRADERS

In Iceland, settlers grabbed as much land as they could, hoping to grow rich and powerful. But Vikings also sought wealth in other ways—by raiding and trading. Tough Viking pirates terrorized peaceful villages and monasteries, snatching treasure and seizing captives. Shrewd Viking traders traveled to fairs and markets, selling rare, valuable goods and everyday essentials.

Sudden, deadly attacks! Viking raiders swooped in from the sea to attack coastal communities throughout Europe. A single lucky raid might make a Viking warrior rich for life!

8

The Iceland national *Thing* met for two weeks every summer. Meetings were led by a Law Speaker and a council of nobles. Laws were not written down, but a third of them were recited out loud each year, so that people would remember them.

Men involved in a quarrel could challenge each other to a duel. The loser was judged to be guilty.

Disputes could be settled peacefully if a wrongdoer agreed to pay his victim a heavy fine.

AROUND AD 972

Oh no! Not again! Hot-tempered Erik the Red has killed another man! Even worse, the murder took place at the yearly meeting of the *Thing* when everyone is meant to be peaceful. Erik bumped into a farmer with whom he had been feuding. They argued and this led to an ugly brawl. Now Erik's enemy is dead! The *Thing* council is furious, and has outlawed Erik.

GREEN AND PLEASANT?

Erik the Red and his companions arrived in Greenland in AD 982. The first Viking settlers there found stark mountains and barren ice sheets. The shallow soil supported little grass and no trees, but the seas teemed with fish and the cliffs housed huge colonies of seabirds. The settlers hunted seals and polar bears for their skins and fur, killed reindeer and whales for meat and blubber (fat), and walrus for their valuable tusks.

Fish drying in the wind (to preserve them to eat in winter)

Erik the Red built a farmhouse at Brattahlid (now Qagssiarssuk) at the southern tip of Greenland.

Nothing remains of the first Viking homes in Greenland. They were probably similar to this house from Iceland.

Woman servant
weaving cloth

Viking women were strong-minded
and independent. They controlled
all household matters, including
managing farms and defending their
families when their menfolk were
away. Many settler families lived in
isolated farmsteads without close
neighbors.

Mother
cooking

Distaff

Metal cooking
pot

Peat fire

Most Viking houses had only one room, used
for working, relaxing, eating, and sleeping. In
Iceland and Greenland, families kept warm by
burning peat (the remains of long-dead plants,
dug from the ground). The hearth (fireplace)
was in the center of each house. It provided
warmth and was also used for cooking.

Grown-up daughter
spinning wool to make
thread

SHIPS AND THE SEA

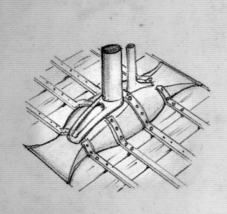

The Vikings were skillful sailors who steered their fast, beautiful ships through the wild, dangerous conditions of the northern seas. From childhood, boys were taught how to row and sail. Viking ships were powered by the wind blowing a single square woolen sail, or by men rowing. They were steered by a large oar at the stern (back).

AROUND AD 997

It must be over two years since I last wrote about Erik the Red and his family. The twenty-five boatloads of settlers that decided to join him from Iceland are still surviving in Greenland. He's had no time for quarreling or fighting since then. Building and farming keep him busy. But his young son, Leif, seems to have inherited his father's energy and ambition. They say he's a promising sailor, too. That young man may go far one day!

Splitting log to make planks

Wedge

Adze

Out at sea, Vikings steered by observing the stars: the Pole Star shows north, and the sun at its highest point in the sky shows south. Seabirds, drifting plants, and animal smells were all signs that land might be near.

Viking sailors all had tales to tell about the mishaps and terrors of their voyages. Going to sea was risky. Even the best ships and most skillful sailors could be lost in a freak accident or sudden storm. Viking storytellers also warned how strange sea monsters—like the Kraken (a giant squidlike creature) or the man-eating Maelstrom (a whirlpool)— could drag sailors down below the waves to their doom.

OVERLAND TRAVEL

It was often easier to travel by sea than to trek across wild country. Long overland journeys were best made in the wintertime. Vikings used sleds, skis, and skates to glide over snow and ice and along frozen rivers.

Ax, used for chopping wood and as a weapon

Forge for heating metal to soften it

Bellows, to pump air into the fire to make it hotter

Anvil, where the smith hammers heated metal into shape

BLACKSMITH'S SKILLS

Each Viking settlement needed a smithy (a blacksmith's workshop), where weapons, farming and woodworking tools, knives, locks, cooking pots, chains, and nails were made and mended. The best weapons and armor were made and decorated by expert craftsmen in towns.

Woman servant
pouring wine

Skald *singing
a poem*

Guest holding
drinking horn

Skalds (royal poets) sang the praises of
kings and entertained guests visiting
royal halls. Viking poems and stories
were not written down, but memorized
and passed on from father to son.

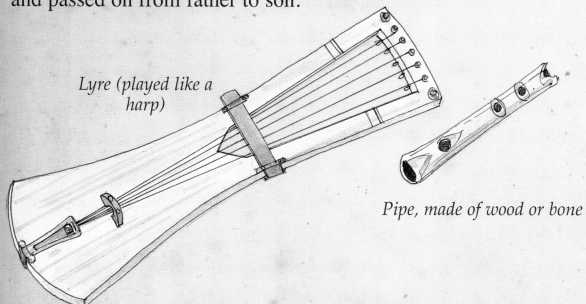

Lyre (played like a
harp)

Pipe, made of wood or bone

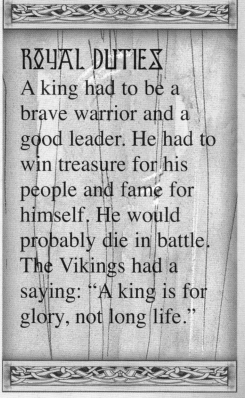

ROYAL DUTIES
A king had to be a
brave warrior and a
good leader. He had to
win treasure for his
people and fame for
himself. He would
probably die in battle.
The Vikings had a
saying: "A king is for
glory, not long life."

OLD GODS, NEW CHURCH

The Vikings believed in many gods and goddesses. Each one watched over a different side of life. Vikings sacrificed animals and people to please the gods and asked for their help and protection.

Vikings liked to wear amulets (lucky charms) shaped like the god Thor's magic hammer.

By around AD 1100, most Vikings had become Christians. But some still believed in the old gods as well.

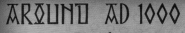

AROUND AD 1000

Young Leif is now back in Greenland, full of new ideas from Norway including a new religion—the Christian faith. He says it was taken there by missionary priests from Germany. Leif tries to encourage his family to become Christians, but Erik the Red is not willing. He's trusted the old Viking gods all his life, and feels it would be dangerous to desert them. Leif's mother wants Erik to build a Christian church. He's not happy!

In AD 922, Ibn Fadlan, a Muslim traveler in Russia, described how Viking merchants he met there said prayers to tall wooden statues of their gods.

Odin was the most powerful Viking god, the wisest, and the most mysterious. He was master of magic, poetry, runes (Viking writing)—but also of battles and madness.

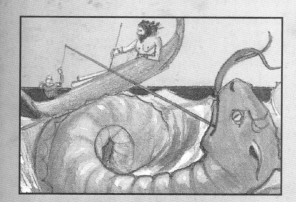

Thor, god of thunder, was big, brave, bold, strong, kindly, hot-tempered, and stupid. He protected Viking farmers and craftsmen, and fought against monsters, such as the fearsome World Serpent.

Loki was a spiteful trickster who was clever, cunning, and malicious. Neither gods nor people could trust him. He gave birth to magic animals, including Odin's eight-legged flying horse, Sleipnir.

The Norns were three veiled goddesses representing past, present, and future. Sitting under Yggdrasil, the holy tree that supported the world, they measured out the threads of life and death for all humans.

Baldur was young and handsome. The other gods loved him and tried to protect him. But evil Loki killed him by a trick—using a sprig of magic mistletoe.

Frigg was the wife of Odin. She was clever and thoughtful. She spent her days spinning airy threads to weave into clouds.

Frey (right) and his sister **Freya** brought new life and love. They gave families many children. They sent rain and sunshine to make farm crops grow.

The Valkyries were wild female warrior-spirits. They flew over battlefields to carry back dead heroes to feast and fight in Odin's palace, Valhalla (the Hall of the Dead).

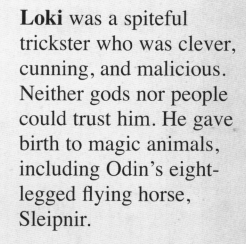

LAND! LAND!

Bjarni Herjolfsson's description of the new land he had seen caused excitement among the Greenland settlers. They had already bravely dared to leave their homes and sail west to settle in an unknown land. Now, many seemed keen to risk another adventure. Bjarni's new land might be better than Greenland.

AROUND AD 1000

I hear that young Leif has set off on another long voyage. He sailed away several weeks ago—into the unknown! This is no ordinary sailing trip to Iceland or Norway. I'm told that Leif bought Bjarni Herjolfsson's ship from him—and set off to find the mysterious land that Bjarni had glimpsed in the storm! He was last seen sailing northwest from Greenland. He's either a fool or a hero. Only time will tell!

Traders, raiders, and explorers all planned their voyages carefully. After choosing a crew—around 35 men—they loaded their ship with all they might need for the voyage. Food, drink, spare sails and oars, and weapons were all essential. Viking ships might also carry trade goods, farm animals, soldiers, or settler women and children.

None of the Viking settlers in Vinland stayed long. Because of quarrels and Skraeling attacks, their houses and farms were deserted by around AD 1015.

DEATH OF THORVALD

Thorvald reached America, and began exploring. He found fine forests, rich grassland, and good weather. He was delighted! But when he came face to face with Skraeling hunters on a beach, he attacked them. One of the Skraeling survivors led an army to fight back. Thorvald was killed by an arrow. He lies buried in America.

LASTING FAME

Leif Eriksson spent the rest of his life on his farm in Greenland, enjoying his memories —and his treasure.

AROUND AD 1020

Just like his father, Leif the Lucky has settled down on dry land. He has no wish to go sailing again or have great adventures. He does not know that he was the first European to land in the vast continent of America. And, unknown to him, the Viking settlements in Greenland will disappear, like his Vinland house, by around AD 1400. Perhaps he still wonders what other lands lie over the ocean, waiting to be explored?

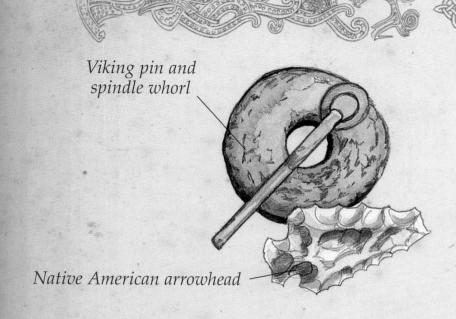

*Viking pin and
spindle whorl*

Native American arrowhead

VIKING REMAINS

In 1961 archeologists discovered the remains of eight Viking houses and a smithy at L'Anse aux Meadows, Newfoundland. Possibly they were built by Viking trader Thorfinn Karlsefni, around AD 1010. They also found a dress pin and a spindle whorl (a weight used in spinning thread) that once belonged to a Viking woman. A stone arrowhead found in Greenland shows that Native American hunters traveled east around the same time as the Vikings were voyaging west.

The saga (history) of Viking settlers in Iceland and Greenland was first written down around AD 1200. At least three different versions survive. About 50 years later, Erik and Leif's story was preserved in two entertaining epics: *The Saga of the Greenlanders* and *The Saga of Erik the Red*.

Thanks to the marvelous memories of skillful storytellers, the exciting adventures of Erik the Red and Leif the Lucky survived without being written down for over 200 years.

Knight: Ready for Battle

Introduction

Travel back in time to medieval Europe, between AD 1000 and 1500. That is when knights built castles, took part in jousts and tournaments, enjoyed hunting and feasting, and fought and died in wars. This period is known as the Middle Ages, because it comes between ancient times and modern times. In the Middle Ages, land was the key to power and wealth—and the land was controlled from the castle. The most powerful person in the land was the king. He allowed nobles to hold land; in return, they promised to fight for him. The nobles in turn gave parts of their land to other knights who agreed to fight for them.

Knights had to swear an oath to be loyal to the king.

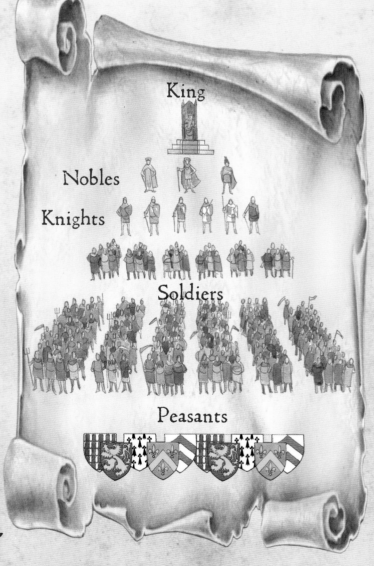

The King's word was law. If he wanted to, he could have you thrown into jail or even beheaded.

34

Training

At the age of 14, when the page had become an esquire, he started to learn fighting techniques.

Quintain

When training with a quintain, the esquire had to hit the target shield then duck quickly, or the swinging weight would knock him off his horse.

Did you know?

Counting the cost
In the 13th century, becoming a knight was so expensive that many young men tried to avoid being knighted and remained esquires.

Did you know?

Wax casts
If an armorer lived a long distance away, a knight might send wax casts of his legs, arms, or torso for new armor to be fitted around.

Light weight
Some suits of armor were light enough for the wearer to be able to run in them, or even do a somersault.

Fully armored

A knight was dressed in his armor by his esquire.

Becoming a Knight

The esquire could hope to become a knight at about the age of 21, once he had successfully completed his training. The night before he was to be knighted, the young esquire was bathed and shaved. Other esquires dressed him in special robes, and he spent the night in prayer. His nighttime vigil over, the young esquire put on his best clothes. His family and friends were waiting in the great hall of the castle, where the ceremony of dubbing would take place.

Coat of arms

A coat of arms was useful for identifying knights in a tournament or in war (see pages 46–47).

Knight school

Wooden swords were used at first to practice sword-fighting.

Did you know?

The Knights Hospitalers were also monks who looked after the sick. They were founded in Jerusalem in the 11th century to look after Christian pilgrims.

38

Bathing

Water was heated on a fire and poured into a wooden tub.

Did you know?

The Templars

The Knights Templars were originally formed to protect Christian pilgrims who visited the Middle East. During the Crusades the Hospitalers and the Templars fought against the Saracens.

The knight's vigil

The young esquire was expected to pray all night for guidance on how to be a good knight.

The ceremony of dubbing a knight

The young esquire knelt before his king or lord, who tapped him on the neck with a sword. This tapping was called an accolade. He was then given his own sword and spurs. This marked his new status as a "gentle, worthy, faithful, and devoted knight," sworn to defend churches, orphans, widows, and "servants of God." The newly dubbed knight then returned to the chapel for a blessing by a priest. The details of the ceremony varied from place to place.

Armor and Weapons

A knight's fighting equipment—which consisted of a sword, a shield, a suit of armor, and a warhorse—was very expensive. Altogether it might cost as much as five farm workers would be paid over twenty years. Well-made armor was almost indestructible; if it was damaged, dents could be hammered out, or broken links of mail repaired.

A. Gauntlet
B. Buckles and hinges

Italian knight, 1385

Arming the knight

It took about an hour for an esquire to dress a knight in his complete suit of armor.

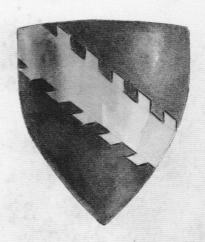

The pattern on this shield is called a bend raguly. (See page 46 for more examples of shield patterns.) Sometimes a small round shield called a buckler was used instead.

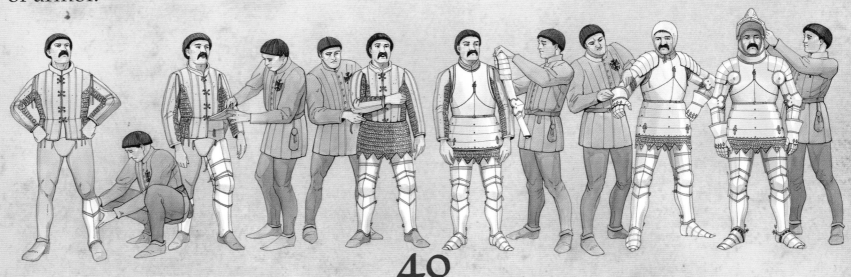

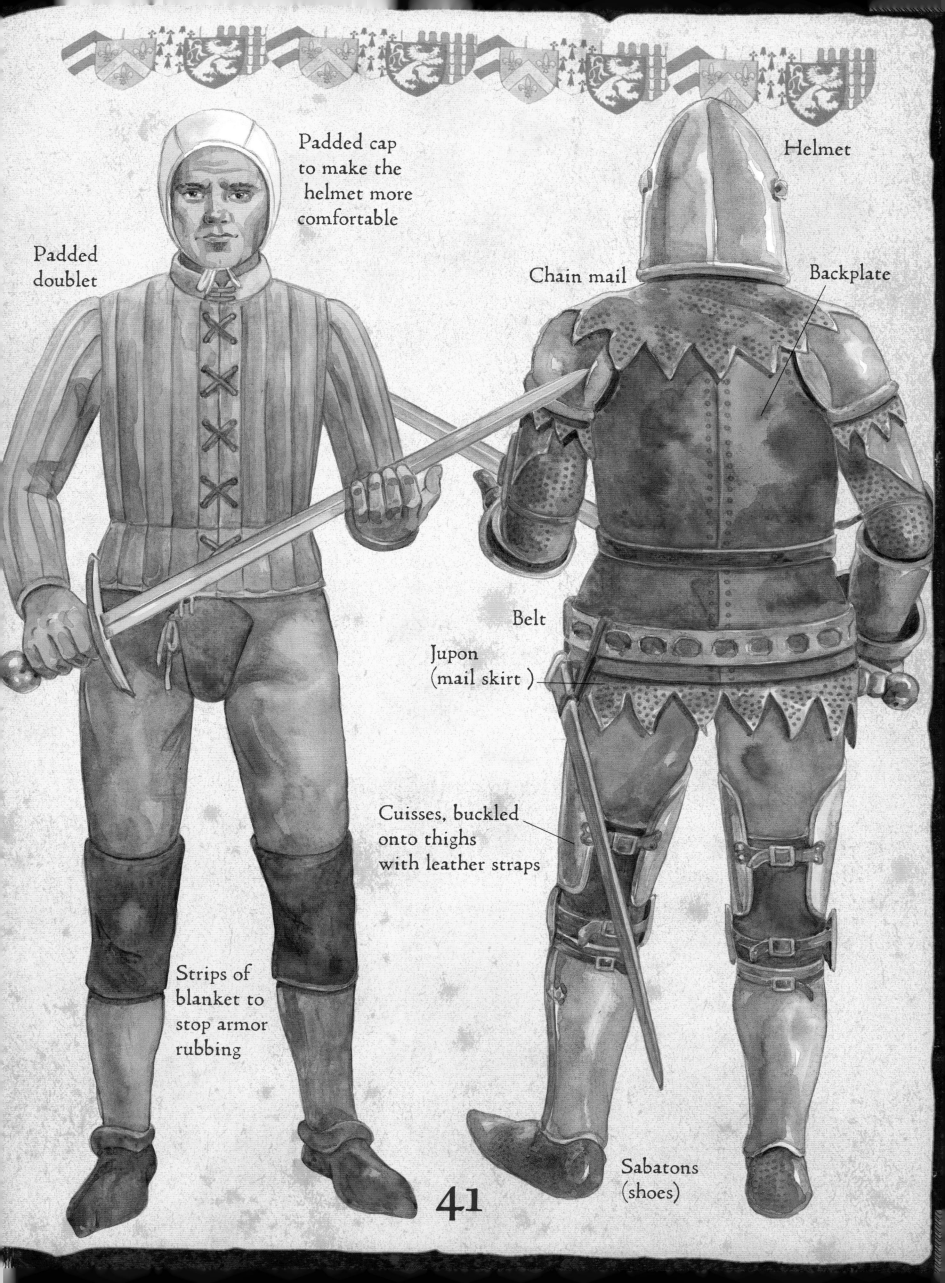

Padded cap
to make the
helmet more
comfortable

Padded
doublet

Helmet

Chain mail

Backplate

Belt

Jupon
(mail skirt)

Cuisses, buckled
onto thighs
with leather straps

Strips of
blanket to
stop armor
rubbing

Sabatons
(shoes)

41

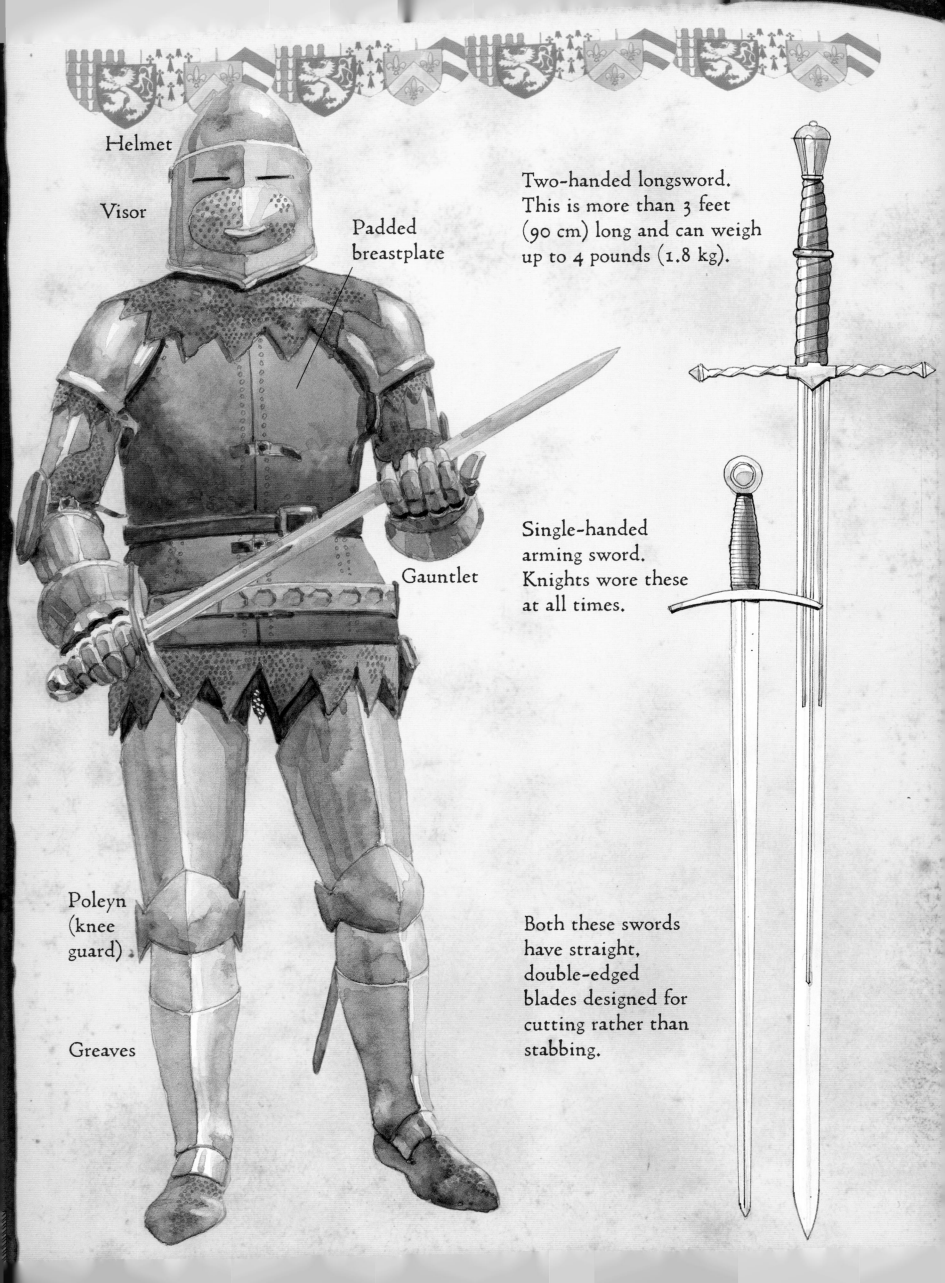

Helmet

Visor

Padded
breastplate

Gauntlet

Poleyn
(knee
guard)

Greaves

Two-handed longsword.
This is more than 3 feet
(90 cm) long and can weigh
up to 4 pounds (1.8 kg).

Single-handed
arming sword.
Knights wore these
at all times.

Both these swords
have straight,
double-edged
blades designed for
cutting rather than
stabbing.

Mail hood

Pauldron

Vambrace

Couter

Pommel

Cantle

Crupper

The right horse for the job

By the thirteenth century, knights usually had at least two warhorses: a courser and a destrier. The courser was a swift hunting horse; the destrier was used for jousting. For traveling, knights and ladies preferred more gentle horses called palfreys. Packhorses, known as sumpter horses, were used to carry baggage.

The pommel and cantle of the saddle make it difficult for the knight to be knocked off his horse.

Spur

Scabbard or sheath

Girth

Stirrup

Gilded spurs were a badge of honor, awarded for an act of bravery.

The spiked wheel at the back of the spur is called a *rowel*.

Heraldry

I n the heat of battle, when knights were encased from top to toe in armor, how could you see who your friends or enemies were? It became especially difficult after the introduction of the closed helmet, which hid a man's face. A system of badges developed, called heraldry. The idea may have come from the Saracens; certainly badges began to be used during the Crusades. Designs known as coats of arms were painted on shields, and later sewn onto the knight's surcoat (a cloth garment worn on top of the armor) and horse trappings.

To begin with, only lords and knights had coats of arms. At first each knight had his own design, but later they became hereditary badges to be handed down in the family.

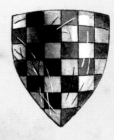

Checky

Chief embattled

Per pale indented

Cross engrailed

Pale   Chief   Bend   Cross   Per fesse

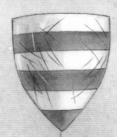

Per saltire   Per cross   Per pale   Paly   Barry

Dividing the shield

The basic shield shape can be divided in many different ways, each of which has its own name. Here are some of the most important designs.

Winning battles

Battles were won by knights and archers fighting together in an intelligent plan. Much was at stake: defeat might mean the loss of an army, or a crown. The enemy foot soldiers would not be any match for a fully arrmored knight charging.

Losing battles

Ordinary soldiers captured by the enemy might be killed or deliberately maimed as a warning to others. Knights, however, were usually taken alive and held for ransom. All knights thought of other knights as equals, who deserved to be treated in a chivalrous way.

Did you know?

There was a kind of arrow that could go right through a knight's armor. The slim "bodkin" arrowheads could pierce mail and kill horses at over 300 feet (90 m). Closer up, they punched straight through plate armor.

53

The Crusades

Siege of Antioch, 1098

In 1071 the Seljuk Turks conquered much of the Byzantine Empire. Fearing that they might conquer Europe, Pope Urban II called for a Christian army to capture Jerusalem. The Church thought that a "holy war" would be a good way of keeping warlike knights occupied. At this time there were two different men claiming to be Pope. Organizing a crusade would give Urban an advantage over his rival.

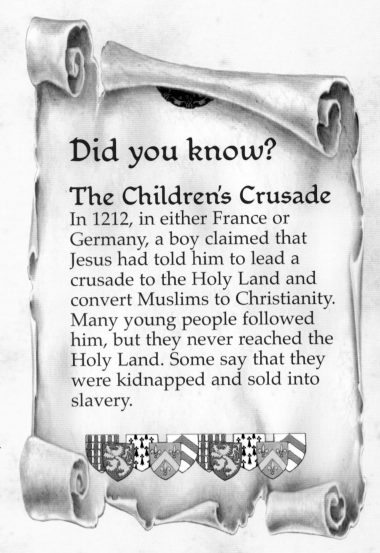

Did you know?

The Children's Crusade
In 1212, in either France or Germany, a boy claimed that Jesus had told him to lead a crusade to the Holy Land and convert Muslims to Christianity. Many young people followed him, but they never reached the Holy Land. Some say that they were kidnapped and sold into slavery.

This is how a European artist imagined Jerusalem in the 15th century.

Why Jerusalem?

Jerusalem is important to Christians, Muslims, and Jews. Christians believe that Jesus preached there and died there on the Cross. Muslims honor Jerusalem as the place where the Prophet Muhammad received a revelation of Heaven. For Jewish people, Jerusalem is the site of their holiest temple, and their traditional home. From AD 750 it had been controlled by Muslim rulers based in Baghdad, in present-day Iraq. For centuries they had allowed Jews and Christians to live there alongside Muslim citizens, but now the Christians felt that this was not enough.

The Esquire's Handbook

Vol. IV

DINING IN THE GREAT HALL

Trenchers

The Lord and his honored guests used plates made of silver. Everyone else ate from big slices of stale bread called trenchers. These soaked up all the grease from the food. Used trenchers were given to the poor.

At night the tables and benches were folded away and the servants slept on straw mattresses on the floor.

Canopy

High table

Lord of the castle

Dais

Scraps were thrown on the floor for the dogs.

Medicine

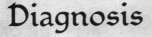

Uroscopy chart

The life of a knight was full of danger. Even when he was not at war, he ran the risk of being seriously injured while jousting or hunting. Wounded knights were sent to surgeons who stopped bleeding by using red-hot irons to cauterize (scorch) a wound. They also sealed wounds with tar. Blood poisoning and a slow death often followed.

Bloodletting

Many diseases were thought to be caused by having too much blood in the body, and the cure was to let some of it out. This could be done by cutting the patient with a knife, or by using leeches (a kind of worm) to suck out the excess blood.

Diagnosis

Since ancient times, doctors have diagnosed illnesses by examining the patient's urine. In medieval plays and stories, the doctor with his specimen bottle is often a figure of fun.

A chart like the one shown above told the doctor how to interpret the urine specimen.

Cutting a hole in the skull (trepanning) was believed to cure various illnesses.

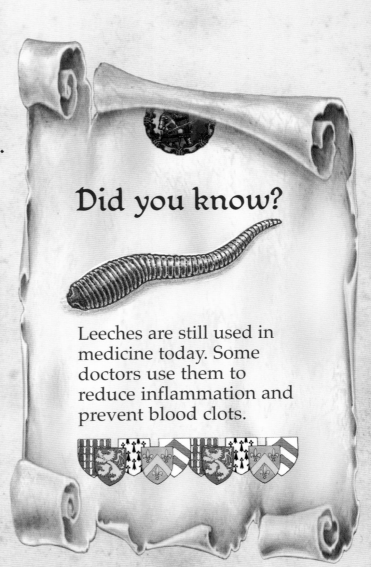

Did you know?

Leeches are still used in medicine today. Some doctors use them to reduce inflammation and prevent blood clots.

Knightly Pastimes

Hunting was a knight's favorite way of staying in shape. Deer were hunted on horseback, with dogs, and kings had their own royal deer parks and reserves where no one could hunt without permission.

A favorite form of hunting for both knights and ladies was hawking or falconry, where wild birds of prey were trained to catch other birds.

Jesses

A hawk in flight. Leather straps called jesses are used to tether the hawk.

A good read

Both knights and ladies enjoyed poems and stories. They would either read these themselves, or have them read or sung, perhaps by a professional musician or "minstrel." Knights could listen to warlike stories about famous heroes such as Roland and Oliver. Ladies might prefer the more romantic tales of King Arthur and his knights. Love songs were popular, and writing them was considered a suitable pastime for a nobleman —even a king.

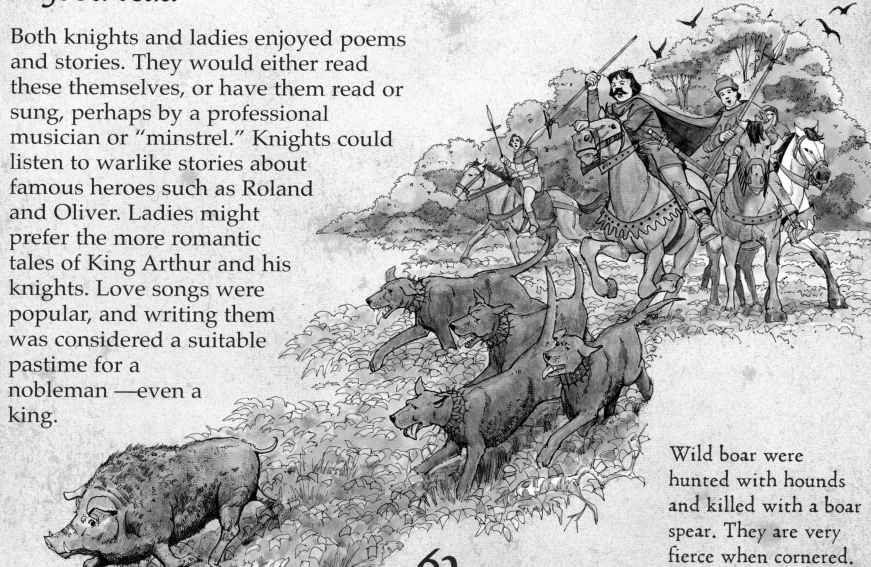

Wild boar were hunted with hounds and killed with a boar spear. They are very fierce when cornered.

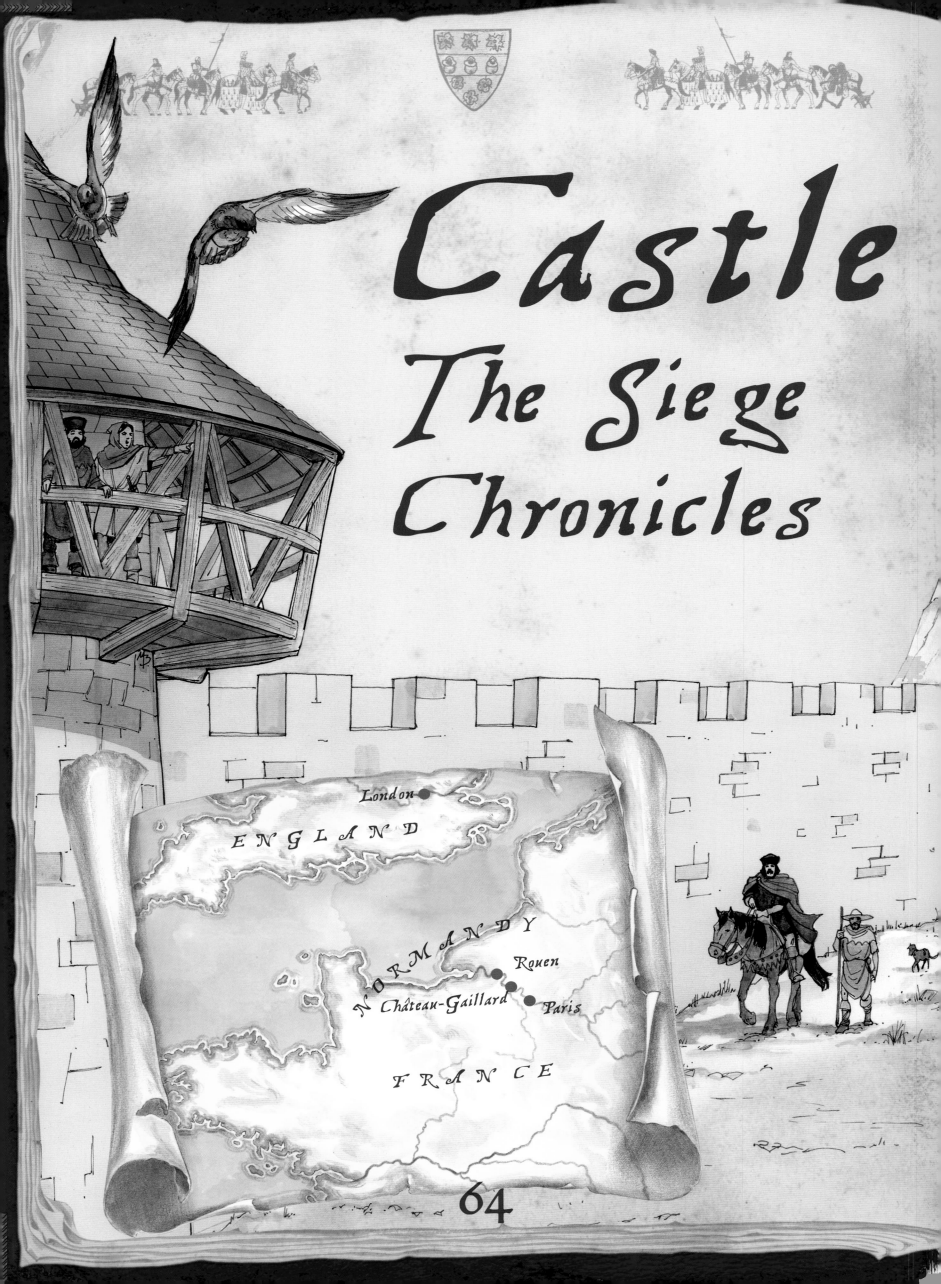

Castle
The Siege Chronicles

London

ENGLAND

NORMANDY

Rouen

Château-Gaillard   Paris

FRANCE

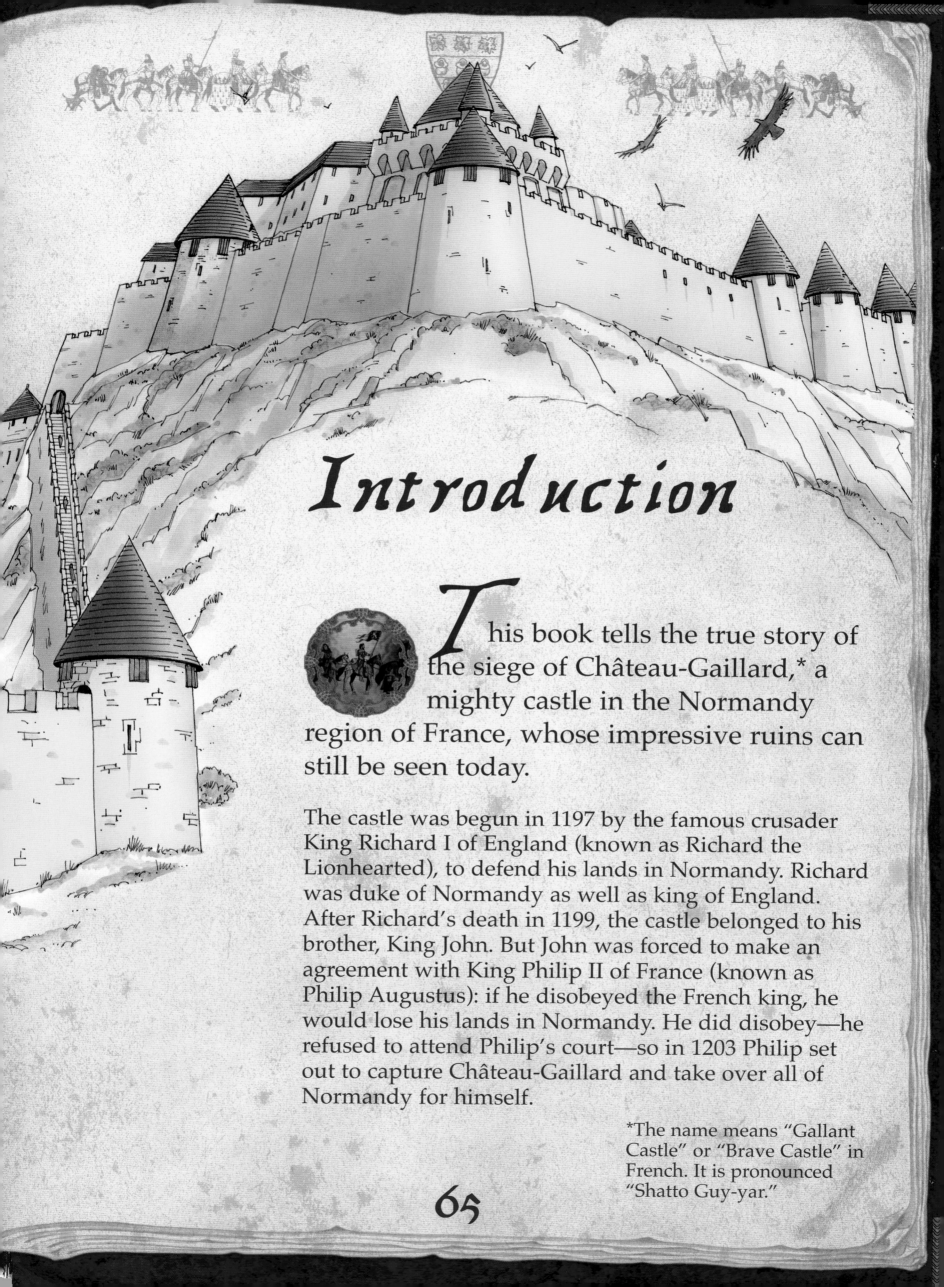

Introduction

This book tells the true story of the siege of Château-Gaillard,* a mighty castle in the Normandy region of France, whose impressive ruins can still be seen today.

The castle was begun in 1197 by the famous crusader King Richard I of England (known as Richard the Lionhearted), to defend his lands in Normandy. Richard was duke of Normandy as well as king of England. After Richard's death in 1199, the castle belonged to his brother, King John. But John was forced to make an agreement with King Philip II of France (known as Philip Augustus): if he disobeyed the French king, he would lose his lands in Normandy. He did disobey—he refused to attend Philip's court—so in 1203 Philip set out to capture Château-Gaillard and take over all of Normandy for himself.

*The name means "Gallant Castle" or "Brave Castle" in French. It is pronounced "Shatto Guy-yar."

The Castle

Most castles in the Middle Ages were built by kings or by the rich lords who backed them.

War and peace

In peacetime, the castle's towers and walls were a sign of the owner's power. The people felt as if the king or lord himself was watching everything that happened in his land.

In times of war, the castle was a safe base for the lord's supporters as they fought their enemies.

The commander of Château-Gaillard was Baron Roger de Lacy. If he had kept a diary of the siege, this is what he might have written.

July 1203

The French are coming! My spies tell me King Philip's army will be here within the week. I have fewer than 200 fighting men; the French have many times that number. If we face them on the battlefield, we will be cut to pieces. Our only hope is to fight from inside the castle. My men are searching the countryside for the food and weapons we need. King John's orders are to defend the castle at all costs. I pray God will give us the strength to succeed.

Hoarding or hourde

Fortified bridge to main castle

Stable

Treadmill to operate crane

Bastion defending main approach to castle

The site

The best places to build a castle were on a hill, at the edge of a cliff, or overlooking the sea or a river. These natural defenses made direct attack almost impossible. Château-Gaillard was built on a bend of the River Seine. It was thought that it could withstand any attack.

Map labels: River Seine · Village (Les Andelys) · Keep · Cliff · Fortified bridges · Inner bailey · Outer bailey · Outwork or bastion

Illustration labels: Inner gateway with portcullis · Keep or donjon · Inner curtain wall · Outer bailey or enceinte · Outer curtain wall · Mill tower · Drawbridge · Scaffolding made from wooden poles tied together

Building the castle

More than 6,000 workers helped to build Château-Gaillard. Amazingly, it took them not much more than a year (1197–1198).

Walls of iron, walls of butter

According to legend, King Philip of France boasted that he could capture Château-Gaillard even if the walls were made of iron.

King Richard replied that he could defend it even if they were made of butter!

The Siege Begins

Attacking a strongly built castle was not easy. The massive stone walls could stand up to most weapons, and the defenders had a commanding view of the countryside all around. Attackers might try to take the castle by surprise, or to bribe the defenders out by offering them money. Only once everything else had been tried did the attackers settle down to besiege the castle.

What is a siege?

The purpose of siege warfare was to cut off the castle from the outside world. The besieging army surrounded the castle so that no one could get in or out. They knew that if the defenders could not get food into the castle they would have to surrender or starve.

Stocking up

When a siege was expected, men were sent out from the castle to buy, borrow, or steal all the food they could find. Then they raised the drawbridges and barred the gates to keep the attackers out. If the defenders were well prepared, they might be able to last out until help came, or until the attackers gave up.

Who lived here?

The lord and his family

Officials: reeve, clerks, priest, marshal

Fighting men: knights, archers, crossbowmen

Entertainers: jugglers, jesters, musicians

The Diary of Roger de Lacy

August 1203

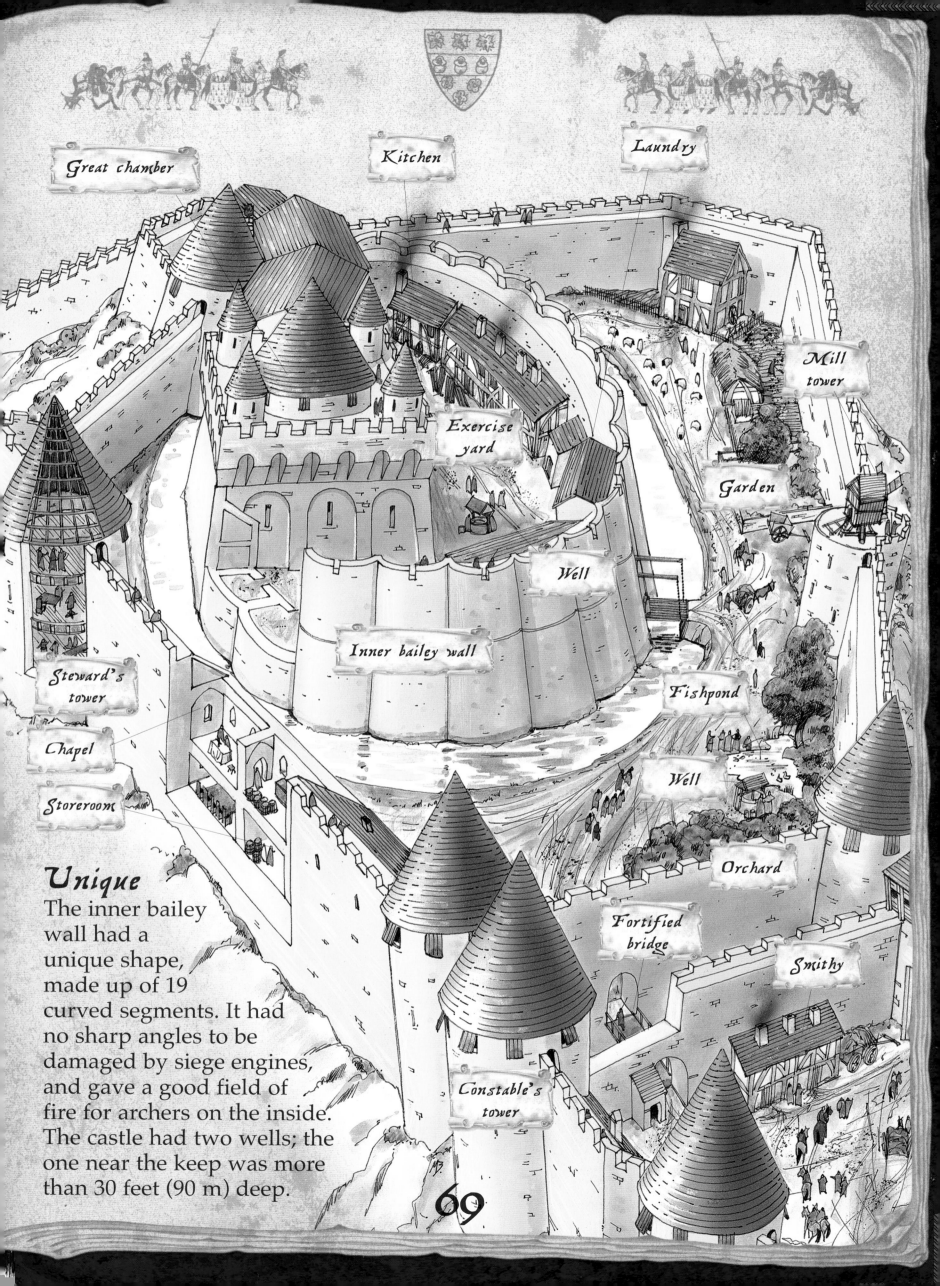

Great chamber

Kitchen

Laundry

Mill tower

Exercise yard

Garden

Well

Inner bailey wall

Steward's tower

Fishpond

Chapel

Well

Storeroom

Orchard

Unique

The inner bailey wall had a unique shape, made up of 19 curved segments. It had no sharp angles to be damaged by siege engines, and gave a good field of fire for archers on the inside. The castle had two wells; the one near the keep was more than 30 feet (90 m) deep.

Fortified bridge

Smithy

Constable's tower

69

Castle Life

Castles weren't just fortresses to be defended or attacked; they were also places where people lived and worked. They were the homes of powerful lords and ladies, sometimes even kings and queens. Inside their massive walls and towers were all the comforts that such important people expected.

Personal hygiene

Medieval people did their best to keep clean—we know that they washed their hands before meals, for example. But the effort of drawing water from the well and heating it meant that even important people bathed only occasionally.

September 1203

Curse the day that King John put the wretched Earl of Pembroke in charge of the army sent to relieve us!

The plan was to strike the French army from two sides at once. One force was to attack overland while the other sailed up the river and attacked from behind. But by the time the English ships arrived, the French had already defeated the land attack. Then their soldiers turned around and fought off the attack from the river.

Now we will have to wait weeks, or even months, for King John to come to our aid a second time.

Holding the fort

When Château-Gaillard was besieged, its owner King John was not there. He was in Rouen, the capital of Normandy, about 25 miles (40 km) away. It was usual for kings to move around, visiting different parts of their lands.

When the lord of a castle wasn't at home, a trusted lieutenant stayed behind with a garrison of soldiers. A castle could never be left undefended!

John sent the Earl of Pembroke with an army to try to relieve the castle, but did not go there himself.

Solar (private upstairs room)

Library

Storerooms

The lord's bed
After his horses and armor, a lord's bed was usually his most valuable possession. It was certainly the most expensive piece of furniture in the castle.

Master bedroom

Wardrobe

Bedroom

Spinning and weaving rooms

Home comforts
The living quarters in a castle were not the empty rooms with bare stone walls that we see today. Walls were neatly plastered and either painted or hung with expensive tapestries.

Wattle and daub

Ordinary buildings were made of oak frames, filled in with panels of "wattle and daub." Wattles are made by weaving together rods and strips of oak. Daub is a kind of plaster made from clay and straw, sometimes with lime or cow dung. The daub makes the walls reasonably waterproof.

Wattle

Thatch

Oak frame

Daub

Pottery jar for
wine, oil, etc.

Brushwood
for fire

Pastrycook

Geese from the
castle yard

Water from
the well

The medieval menu

In peacetime, wealthy people ate mostly meat, including game which they had hunted themselves. The poor lived mostly on things made from grain: bread, porridge, and weak beer.

Making it last

As the siege went on, the castle cooks' job became more difficult, because there was no way of keeping food fresh. Butter and cheese made from milk kept quite well, although sometimes the cheese grew too hard to cut. Fruit and vegetables had to be pickled or dried if they were to last more than a couple of weeks. Meat was smoked or salted, but this did not stop it going rotten, so the cooks might need to use strong spices and herbs to hide any nasty taste. Sometimes, by the end of a long siege, the defenders had nothing left to eat but moldy bread and rats.

The Poor in War

Most castles had a village nearby. The people who lived there grew the crops which fed the people at the castle. They were serfs, which meant that they had very few rights and were almost owned by the local lord. In return, it was, in theory, his duty to protect them when they were in danger.

The peasants' lot

It's always the poor that suffer! In wartime, soldiers often attacked villages and towns, and took food and anything else of value that they found. Sometimes they even burned down the houses. The villagers could not fight back, so they sheltered in the castle grounds. But feeding hundreds of villagers meant that the castle's food ran out more quickly. Because of this, villagers were often driven out of the castle—and that is what Roger de Lacy did. He called them "useless mouths."

December 1203

The siege has lasted four months now, and as we get deeper into winter our supplies of food grow low. Some weeks ago I had to turn the remaining villagers out of the castle. This time the French did not let them pass. They drove them back to the castle gates, but I dared not let them in again. We cannot afford to feed useless mouths! The poor wretches were stuck between us and the French. They had no food, no water, and no shelter from the freezing winter weather. It was only after many had died from starvation and cold that Philip let them pass. Not that they had anywhere to go—their homes have probably been burned down.

Soldiers loot the village below the castle

Those who resist are likely to be killed

Peasant life

The life of a medieval peasant was tough. They worked long hours in the fields just to keep themselves from going hungry, and a portion of what they grew was taken by the lord of the manor as rent.

Lost in no-man's-land

If the besiegers wouldn't let them pass, then the wretched men, women, and children turned out of the castle were trapped in the open without food or shelter. Their only hope was to stay alive until one side or the other finally took pity on them.

Fighting Men

There were very few full-time soldiers in the Middle Ages. Kings and other lords had a small band of troops to protect them, and every castle had a garrison of trained fighting men who kept it safe from surprise attack. It was only in times of war that large armies were raised.

Leaving home to train as a knight

Knights and foot soldiers

Knights were the elite fighters in a medieval army. They rode horses, wore armor, and could fight either on horseback or on foot. They were highly trained and spent a lot of time practicing their fighting skills.

Archers were also highly skilled, but, like ordinary foot soldiers, most of them were only called up into the army when they were needed. In peacetime they were farmers who worked on the land. Their fields had to be plowed, seeds sown, and crops harvested. If any of those things weren't done, people would starve. Sometimes a siege had to be called off simply because it was time for the attacking army to return to their fields to work.

Haqueton (padded jacket)

Longbow made of yew wood

Quiver of arrows

Archer

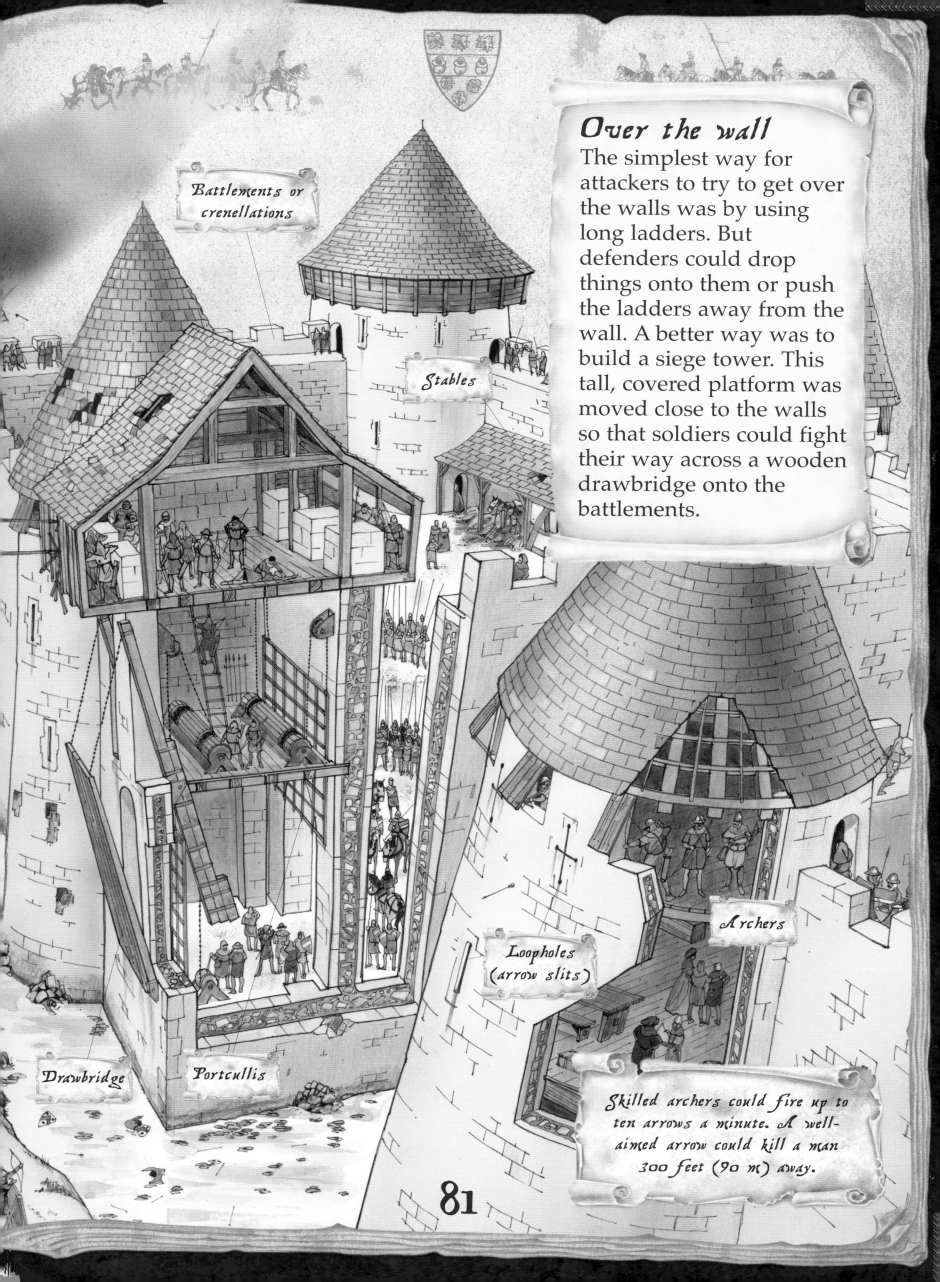

Battlements or crenellations

Stables

Over the wall

The simplest way for attackers to try to get over the walls was by using long ladders. But defenders could drop things onto them or push the ladders away from the wall. A better way was to build a siege tower. This tall, covered platform was moved close to the walls so that soldiers could fight their way across a wooden drawbridge onto the battlements.

Loopholes (arrow slits)

Archers

Drawbridge

Portcullis

Skilled archers could fire up to ten arrows a minute. A well-aimed arrow could kill a man 300 feet (90 m) away.

81

Bombardment

Castle walls were immensely strong, up to 10 feet (3 m) thick. It was not easy to break them down, but it could be done. Before cannons were invented, army engineers built huge siege engines—machines made from wood and ropes, which could fling heavy missiles a surprisingly long way. Mangonels and trebuchets throwing heavy stones were the most common siege engines. The attackers used them to batter the castle wall, hoping to weaken it until eventually part of it fell down.

One week later

Today is the sixth day that the French have battered our outer walls with rocks from their siege engines. But in spite of all their efforts, not the slightest crack has appeared. No wonder that this afternoon they loaded one of their engines with the rotting bodies of two dead horses. Then they hurled them over the wall into the outer bailey. Perhaps they have finally realized that they are wasting their time trying to smash through our wall. Instead they hope to infect us with some monstrous disease from the rotting horses. That will fail as well, I trust. A few more weeks and they will give up and go away—if we can only last out that long.

The ballista
The ballista, first invented by the ancient Greeks, was like a huge crossbow, firing giant arrows or "bolts."

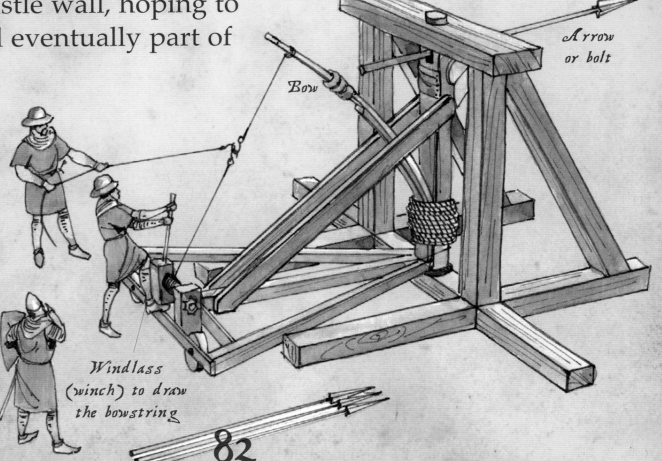

Bow

Arrow or bolt

Windlass (winch) to draw the bowstring

82

The mangonel

A rock was loaded into the cup on the end of the arm, then the arm was pulled back. When it was released it shot forward, catapulting the rock into the distance.

Rock

Padding to protect crossbar

Twisted sinew

A twisted rope made of animal sinew provided the power for the mangonel.

Sling

Arm

The trebuchet

This worked like a giant slingshot.

Weight

The end of the arm was pulled down and the rock was loaded in the sling pouch. When the arm was released, the weight of the box of stones at the far end shot the rock into the air.

Mining the Walls

Even after weeks of bombardment by mangonels and trebuchets, a castle wall might still not fall. That's why attackers often mined underneath it as well. The idea was to weaken the wall's foundations until part of it fell down. Philip decided to use this method to get into the advance bastion—the separate, small castle that guarded the entrance to Château-Gaillard.

Sappers

The soldiers who dug mines were called sappers. They were usually men who had worked in lead or gold mines. Any kind of mining was dangerous, because the roof could easily fall in and kill everyone inside. But undermining a castle wall was even worse, because the defenders were trying to kill you while you did it. They might flood the mine with water and drown the miners. Or they might dig a tunnel of their own (a countermine) so they could go down and drive the miners out.

Two days later

I never thought it possible! Today part of the wall of the outer bastion collapsed. The French sappers had tunneled underneath it without our knowing. Yesterday they set fire to the wooden props supporting it. Even then the wall stood firm. But this morning their siege machines struck the undermined wall with one boulder after another, and finally it fell. Before the French could scramble in over the rubble, I gave orders to set fire to everything in the outer bastion. In the smoke and confusion we retreated to the outer bailey of the main castle. Its walls are higher and stronger, and we should be safe here. We have lost a battle, but I know we can still win the war.

Munitions

Arrowheads were made in many different styles, from narrow "bodkins" to wide heads with barbs. Some were specially hardened and may have been able to pierce chain mail.

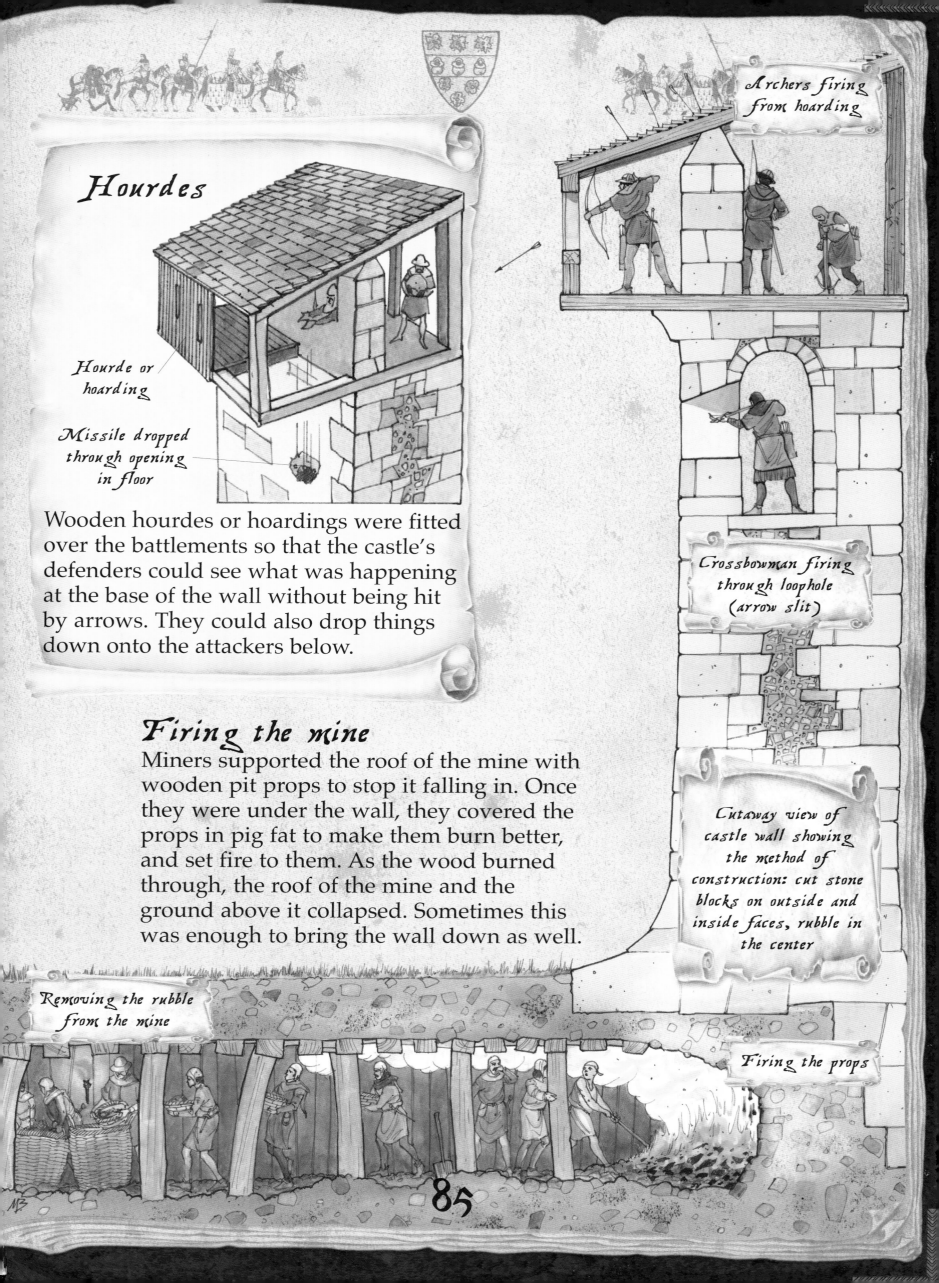

Hourdes

Hourde or hoarding

Missile dropped through opening in floor

Wooden hourdes or hoardings were fitted over the battlements so that the castle's defenders could see what was happening at the base of the wall without being hit by arrows. They could also drop things down onto the attackers below.

Firing the mine

Miners supported the roof of the mine with wooden pit props to stop it falling in. Once they were under the wall, they covered the props in pig fat to make them burn better, and set fire to them. As the wood burned through, the roof of the mine and the ground above it collapsed. Sometimes this was enough to bring the wall down as well.

Archers firing from hoarding

Crossbowman firing through loophole (arrow slit)

Cutaway view of castle wall showing the method of construction: cut stone blocks on outside and inside faces, rubble in the center

Removing the rubble from the mine

Firing the props

Praying for Help

Castles in Christian countries had at least one chapel. In larger castles there were often two. The lord and his family worshipped in a small private chapel close to their rooms. This could be highly decorated, with painted walls, gold crosses and candlesticks, and sometimes even stained-glass windows. Everyone else went to services in a bigger chapel, which might be somewhere in the castle grounds. This would be more plainly decorated than the private chapel.

The castle priest

Castles had their own priests who said Mass every day of the week. Priests were important also because they could read and write; many people at this time couldn't even write their own names. Part of the priest's job was reading and explaining the Bible to those who couldn't read it for themselves. He might also help the lord with the many letters and documents he had to deal with.

Religion

Christianity was the main religion in Europe, but Islam was the chief religion in the Middle East. There was longstanding warfare at this time between the followers of these two religions—but there were also plenty of wars between people of the same religion.

The beginning of the end

At Château-Gaillard the main castle chapel was built against the wall of the outer bailey. Inside the chapel there was a "garderobe," or toilet. The waste from the garderobe dropped down through a space, or chute, in the wall and emptied to the outside. It is said that some French soldiers climbed up the garderobe chute into the chapel. Then they climbed out into the outer bailey through a chapel window and let down the drawbridge for the rest of the French troops.

What happened next?

The valiant defenders of Château-Gaillard were spared by the French king and ransomed. King John himself paid 1,000 marks of silver to ransom Roger de Lacy. King John lost Normandy and most of his lands in France. No wonder his nickname was John Lackland.

Roger de Lacy surrenders his sword

A herald announces that the garrison has surrendered

Useful Words

accolade a tap on the neck with a sword; part of the knighting ceremony.

adze an axlike tool used for smoothing and shaping wood.

amulet a charm, sometimes a gemstone, which is said to protect the wearer from harm.

arming sword a one-handed sword with a straight, double-edged blade.

armorer a metalworker who made armor.

bailey the area of ground inside a castle's walls. Château-Gaillard had two sets of walls, forming an inner and an outer bailey.

ballista a siege engine resembling a giant crossbow.

barren unsuitable for growing crops or grazing cattle.

bastion a small fortress attached to a larger one. Because Château-Gaillard could only be attacked from one direction, a bastion was built to protect that side.

battlements the top part of a castle's walls, usually with a walkway on the inside where defenders could stand.

buckler a small circular shield.

charge the main design on a coat of arms, such as a lion or a griffin.

chivalry the knightly code of behavior.

coax to convince by using a good argument.

courser a swift horse for hunting.

crusade a Christian military expedition to the Middle East.

curtain wall a strong outer wall surrounding a castle, with towers along it for defense.

destrier a warhorse.

distaff a thin wooden pole, used in spinning wool or flax, to keep the fibers from tangling.

drawbridge a bridge, usually over a moat or ditch, which can be raised and lowered.

dubbing the ceremony of making an esquire into a knight.

earl a noble chieftain or war leader.

esquire a knight's servant, 14–21 years old, who is training to become a knight himself.

excavation the process of digging up historical artifacts and remains.

falchion a heavy slicing sword with a curved, single-edged blade.

feud a longstanding argument between two groups or families, often leading to violence.

freeman a person who is neither a slave nor a noble.

garderobe a medieval toilet. The waste dropped through a chute in the castle wall.

garrison a troop of soldiers stationed in a castle to protect it from attack.

halberd an infantry weapon which consists of a strong spear with an axlike blade.

hearth a stone-lined fireplace used for cooking and heating.

heraldry the system of badges used to identify knights in battle.

hoarding or **hourde** a wooden shelter for defenders, overhanging the battlements.

hull the main body of a ship.

joust a single combat between two knights who ride toward one another with lances.

keel a large wooden beam, around which the hull of a ship is built.

keep the main tower of a castle; the final place for the defenders to retreat to. The rest of the castle's walls were there to protect the keep.

knarr a merchant ship with a deep, wide hull.

knight a highly trained fighting man who rode a horse and wore armor. He could fight on horseback or on foot. He usually came from a wealthy family, and owned land.

landholding the right to own an unclaimed piece of land.

Law Speaker a wise man who recited the Viking laws to ensure that people remembered them.

longship a Viking warship designed for speed.

longsword a two-handed sword with a straight, double-edged blade.

mangonel a siege machine made from wood and twisted ropes; a kind of catapult.

mêlée a mock combat between two teams of knights.

Middle Ages a modern name for the period between about AD 950 and 1500.

mining or **undermining** digging tunnels under the foundations of a wall to weaken it and help bring it down.

minstrel a professional musician and entertainer; sometimes they were also spies.

missile any kind of weapon that is thrown in some way.

moat a deep ditch, usually filled with water, surrounding all or part of a castle.

noble a person from an important family.

outlaw a person who has been banished from a community for committing crimes.

page a young servant, 7–14 years old, who hopes to become an esquire.

palfrey a horse for everyday riding.

peat the remains of long-dead plants, dug up from the ground. It can be used as a building material or as a fuel.

Pole Star a star that lies directly overhead when viewed from the North Pole.

portcullis a heavy grille, sliding up and down in grooves, that can be used to close a gateway.

quintain a target mounted on a swiveling post, used to practice jousting.

ransom to pay money for a prisoner to be released. This was a normal part of warfare in the Middle Ages.

runes Viking writing; some other civilizations used similar symbols.

saga a long story, often describing a person's entire life.

Saracens the name used by Christians in the Middle Ages to refer to Muslims.

Scandinavia a large region covering present-day Sweden, Denmark, and Norway; sometimes the name is also used to include Finland, Iceland, Greenland, and neighboring islands.

serf a person who farmed land but did not own it. Serfs had few rights and were not much more than slaves to the lords who owned the land.

siege the process of trying to capture a castle or town by surrounding it with troops so that it was totally cut off from the outside world.

siege engine any kind of machine used to attack a castle during a siege.

siege tower a wooden tower that was moved up to a castle's walls so that attacking soldiers could climb across to the battlements.

skald a Viking poet.

skerry a small, rocky island, too small to live on.

Skraelings the Viking name for the inhabitants of "Vinland" (present-day Newfoundland), who traded with the Vikings.

smithy the workplace of a blacksmith.

stern the back end of a ship.

strake a curved wooden plank, part of the hull of a ship.

tinctures the standard colors used in heraldry.

Thing a two-week-long meeting, occurring every summer, where Viking laws were recited and criminals punished.

tournament a sporting contest of mêlées and jousting.

trebuchet a siege engine that worked like a giant slingshot. It was bigger than a mangonel and was developed much later.

trench a narrow ditch, usually with a bank of earth in front of it, where soldiers can shelter from attackers.

Valhalla the Hall of the Dead, in the god Odin's palace, where Vikings believed heroes were taken after death.

vigil a night spent in prayer, before a religious festival or before the dubbing ceremony.

World Serpent the snake that the Vikings believed surrounded the Earth, grasping its own tail.

Yggdrasil the World Tree, a great ash tree located at the center of the universe, according to Viking beliefs.

Index